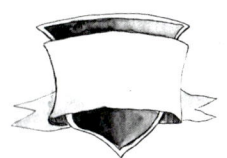

WALT'S ANCESTORS
A Pilgrimage to the Past

Written by Christopher W. Tremblay
Illustrated by Mallary Quinn

Sixth Book in the Walt's Pilgrimage Book Series

Enjoy learning about Walt Disney
Christopher Tremblay

© 2019

Dedicated to Ron Miller

Son-in-Law of Walt Disney

1933-2019

Ron was a friend to Walt's Pilgrimage

Vincit Qui Patitur

He conquers who Endures

"[Dad]…thinks that it's interesting to know just where your family came from. What they did. He was proud that they were good, honest people who worked hard and amounted to something in their own little way…"

Sharon Mae Disney Lund
Daughter of Walt Disney

Walt Disney grew up in a very simple time. He went on to do some amazing things in his life.

This story tells about Walt's family prior to his birth on December 5, 1901.

Get ready to learn about Walt's ancestors and his cultural heritage.

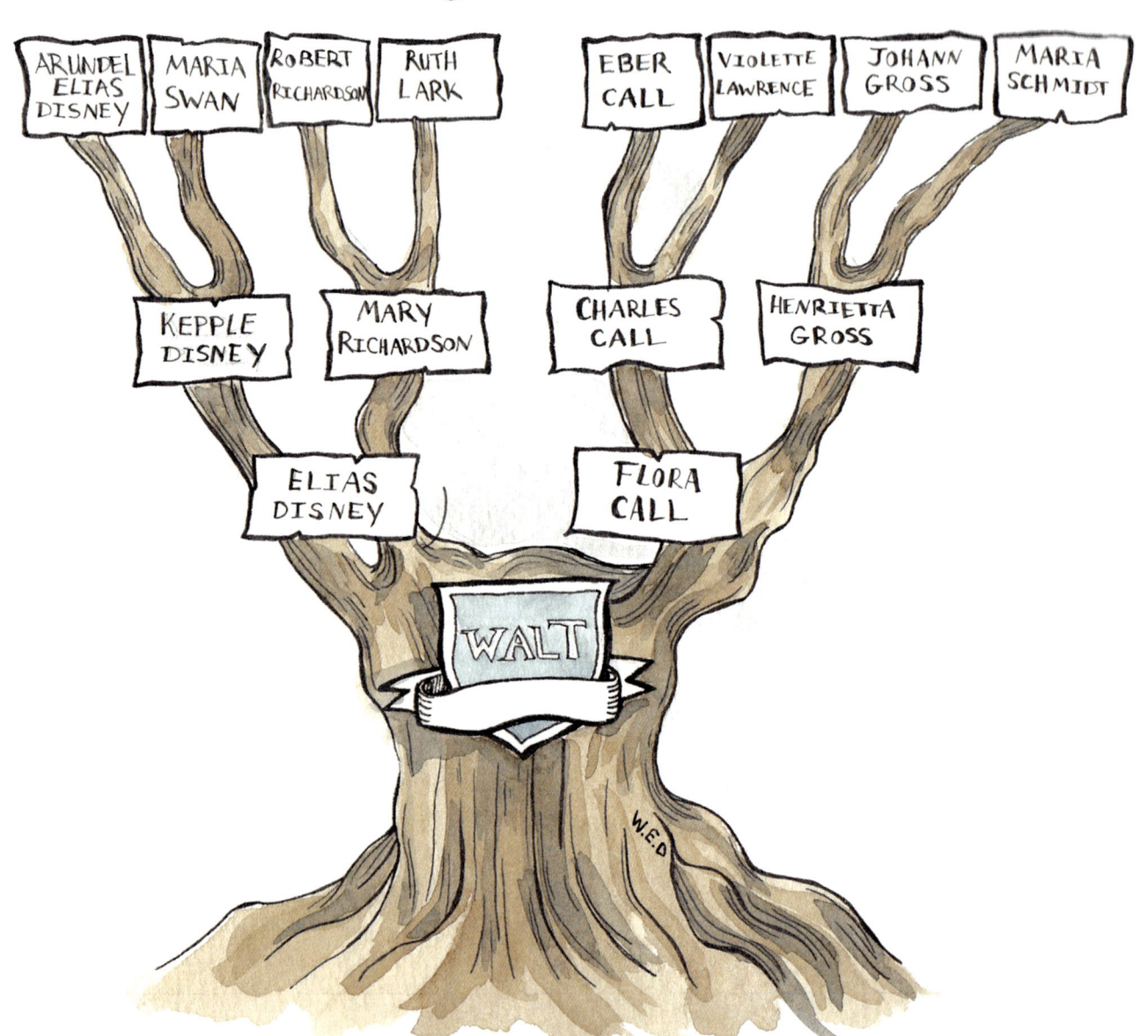

Hughes Suhart fought with William the Conqueror as a knight
But then referred to himself as Hughes d'Isigny as he took flight

Changing your name was a custom of the time
To inform people where you were from, in your lifetime

**From this village, Hughes d'Isigny left with his son
Headed to England, one-by-one**

**Invading Great Britain was their plan
Changing their last name to Disney, they formed a new clan**

In the 1600s, the British monarchy was restored
But the Disneys moved to Ireland,
  where they explored

They settled in County Kilkenny on the
  southeastern side
Surrounded by medieval ruins on the outside

IRISH TRANSLATION
Sna 1600idí, athchóiríodh an monarcacht Briotanach
Ach bhog na Disneys go hÉirinn áit a ndearna siad iniúchadh

Shocraigh siad i gContae Chill Chainnigh ar an taobh thoir theas
Timpeallaithe ag fothracha meánaoiseacha ar an taobh amuigh

In 1801, Arundel Elias Disney was born in Ireland
Thirty three years later, he joined his brother Robert to sail to a new land

To begin a new life in America was the plan
New horizons, they began to scan

After the month's journey, they landed in New York
And the brothers split, each taking a road of a different fork

Arundel Elias Disney was Walt Disney's great grandfather on his father's side.

Kepple had been born in Ireland, you see
He married Irish-born immigrant Mary Richardson with glee

Kepple and Mary settled in nearby Bluevale on 100 acres of land
Where they built a small pine cabin as planned

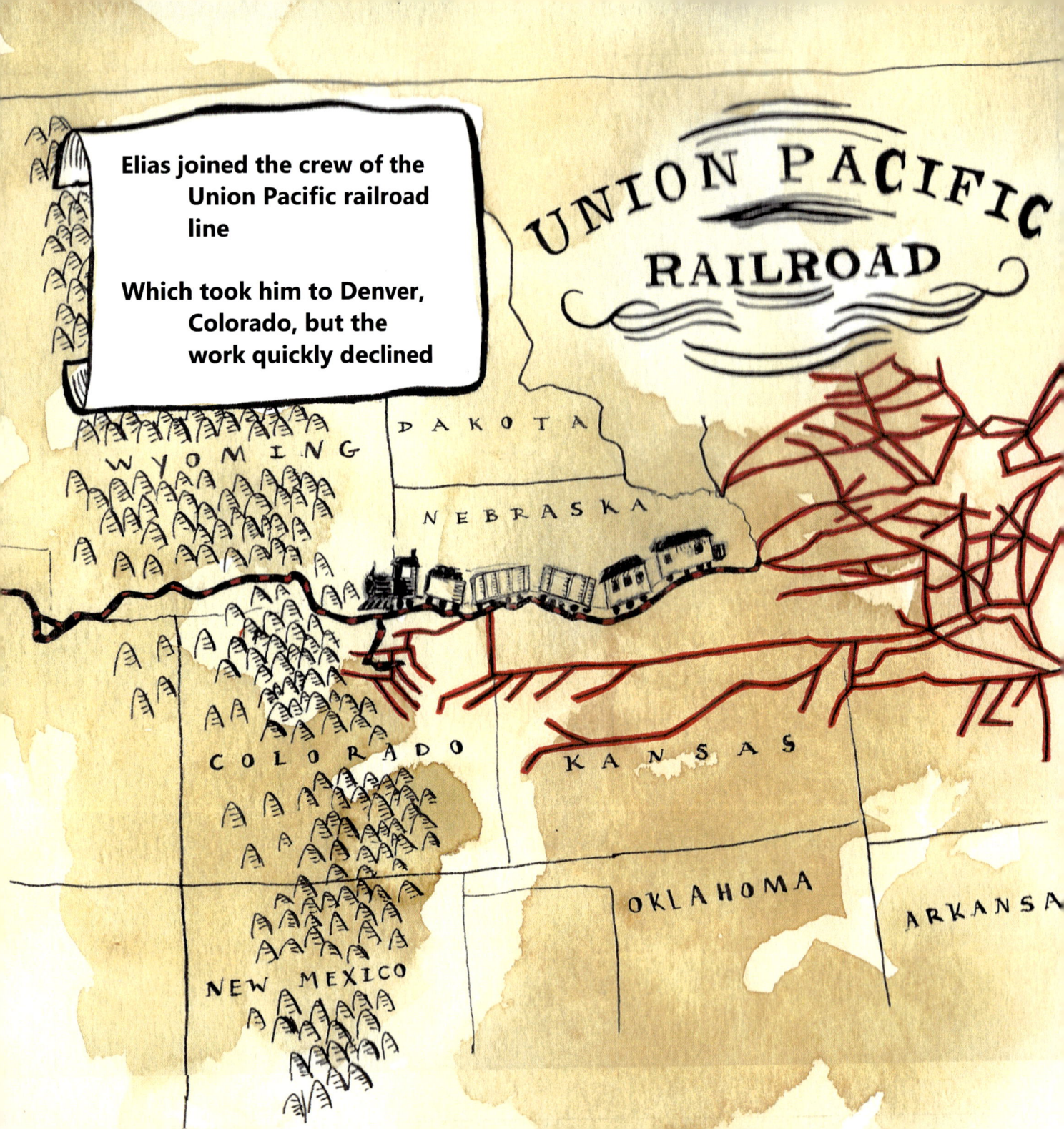

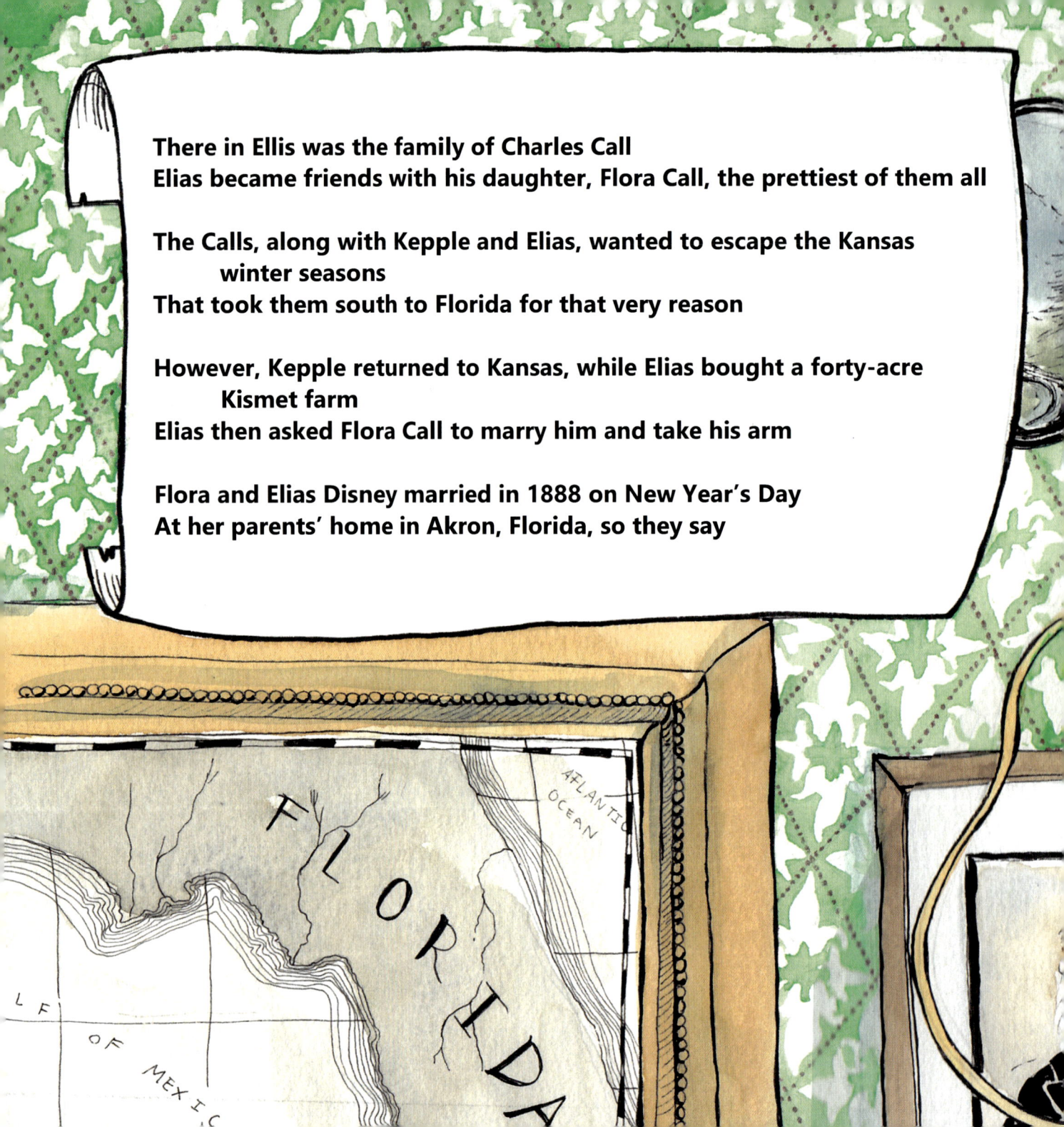

There in Ellis was the family of Charles Call
Elias became friends with his daughter, Flora Call, the prettiest of them all

The Calls, along with Kepple and Elias, wanted to escape the Kansas
    winter seasons
That took them south to Florida for that very reason

However, Kepple returned to Kansas, while Elias bought a forty-acre
    Kismet farm
Elias then asked Flora Call to marry him and take his arm

Flora and Elias Disney married in 1888 on New Year's Day
At her parents' home in Akron, Florida, so they say

It was a two-story house with white and blue trim
It was on the corner and anything but dim

The Disney family grew with two more brothers joining the clan
Raymond and Oliver – all a part of the plan

Walt was named after the local church preacher, Walter Parr
And he was destined to become a legendary star

He was born with Elias' prominent Roman nose
His mother liked to dress up Walt in frilly clothes

D'ISIGNY

That is the story of life before Walt,
dating back in time
Back when Hughes d'Isigny was in his prime

&

Walt Disney went on to become a
man of success and fame
Living 65 years, bringing honor
to the Disney name

DISNEY

According to The Walt Disney Company, the Disney heraldry is:

Coat of Arms: Three gold fleur de lis on a red fess, representing purity or light.

Crest: A red lion passant guardant representing bravery or courage. A crest is a part of the Coat of Arms. Red symbolized a family who served in the military.

Motto: Vincit qui patitur.

Motto Translated: He conquers who endures.

On the door of the Ye Olde Christmas Shoppe in Liberty Square at the Magic Kingdom in Walt Disney World, there is a heart-shaped sign that says Kepple, Est. 1779. The name Kepple is a tribute to Walt's great-great grandfather, Kepple Disney.

Tributes to the Disney Family

In Frontierland (near the Shooting Gallery) at Walt Disney World's Magic Kingdom, there is a burlap sack in a display window and an advertisement that feature "Uncle Kepple and Sons Feed and Farm Supply."

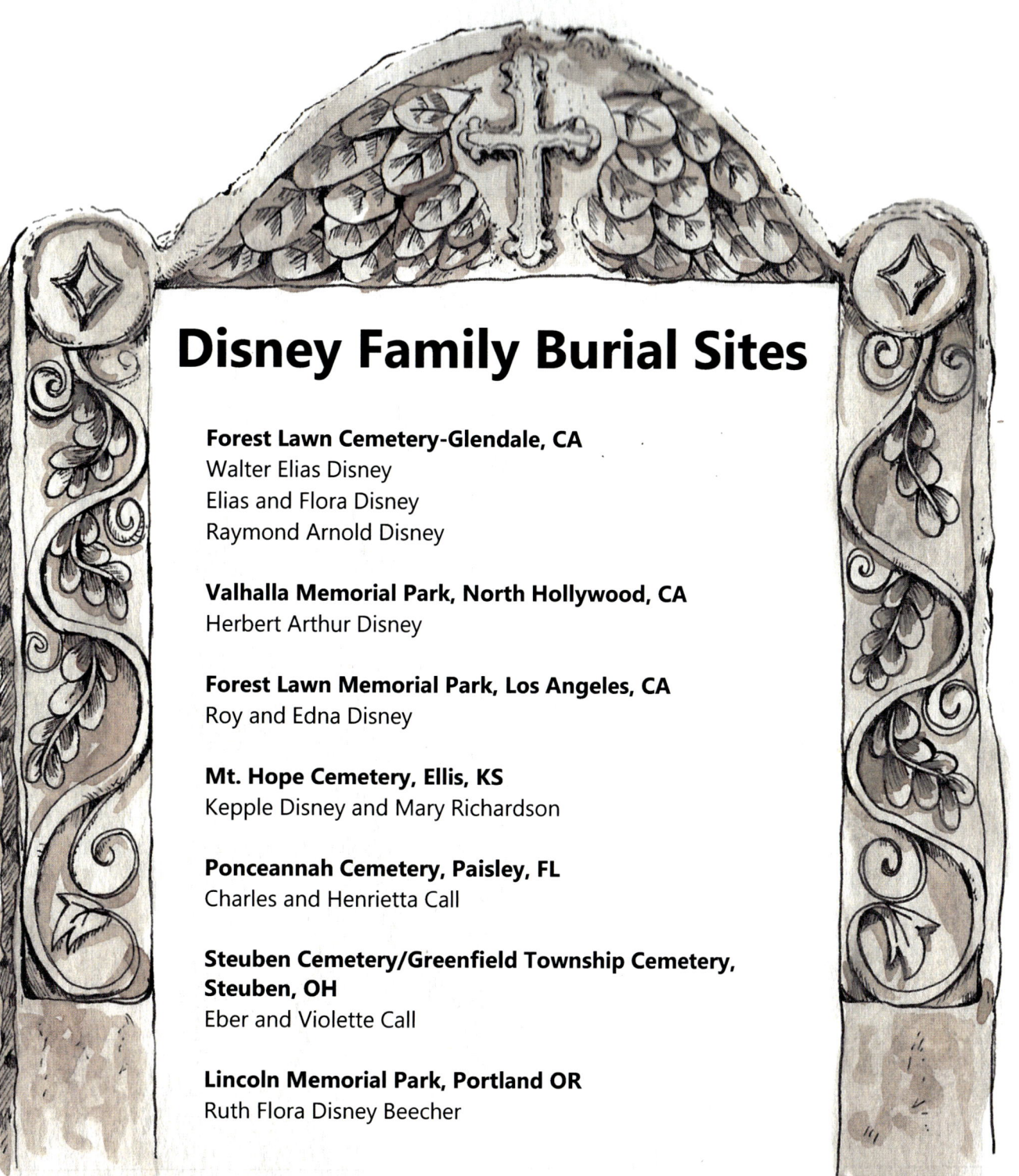

Sources Consulted

Korkis, J. (December 2, 2019). *The Vault of Walt, Christmas Edition.* Volume 7. Theme Park Press.

Korkis, J. (November 24, 2017). *The Disney Coat of Arms.* Retrieved from https://yourfirstvisit.net/2017/11/24/a-friday-visit-with-jim-korkis-the-disney-coat-of-arms/

Thomas, B. (1994). *Walt Disney: An American Original.*

Tremblay, C. (2017). *Walt's Pilgrimage.*

Walt's Pilgrimage Book Series
Created by Dr. Christopher W. Tremblay

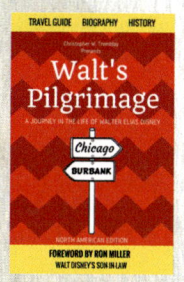 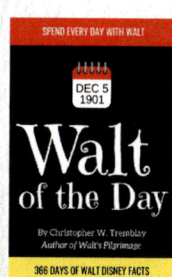  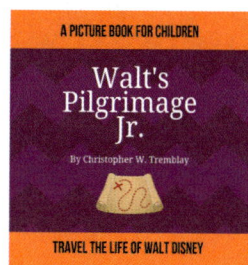 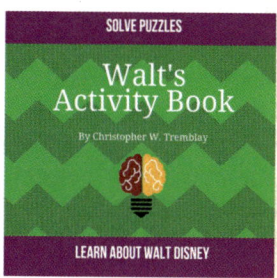

waltspilgrimage.com/walt-book-series

Made in the USA
Lexington, KY
19 June 2019